NEVER GET TOO PERSONALLY INVOLVED WITH YOUR OWN LIFE

By Tom Wilson

Sheed Andrews and McMeel, Inc.
Subsidiary of Universal Press Syndicate
Kansas City

"Ziggy" is syndicated internationally by
UNIVERSAL PRESS SYNDICATE

Copyright © 1975 by

UNIVERSAL PRESS SYNDICATE

ISBN: 0-8362-0623-1
Library of Congress Catalog Card Number 75-16558

for YOU
my "ZIGGY friend

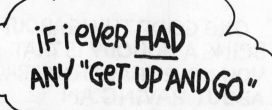

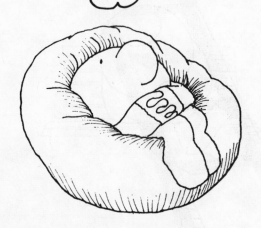

ONE GOOD THING ABOUT
BEING A NOBODY IS THAT
YOU NEVER HAVE TO WORRY
ABOUT HAVING AN
IDENTITY CRISIS...

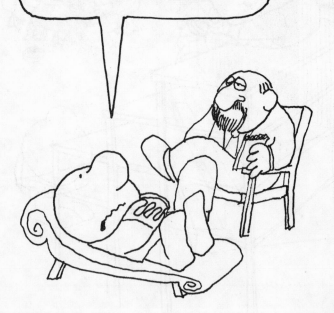

ABOUT THE ONLY THING
THAT HAPPENS TO ME
ON WEEK-ENDS IS...

...i GET TWO DAYS OLDER !!

LIFE'S A LITTLE
LESS COMPLICATED
WHEN YOU
LIVE ALONE.....

FOR ONE THING
THERE'S NEVER
ANY QUESTION
ABOUT WHO
DIDN'T JIGGLE
THE HANDLE ON
THE "JOHN"!!

LIVE LIFE ONE LUMP AT A TIME

...it's been one of <u>those</u> days!!

First i get into a big fight with my wife... then i go out to start the car and find i have a flat tire...

...next i get a parking ticket right outside my own barber shop...

BEWARE
OF

..i GO THROUGH LIFE
WITH THE FEELING THAT
i'M THE ONE WEARING
THE "KICK ME" SIGN..

..YOU KNOW YOU'RE "OUT OF IT"
WHEN YOU CAN'T RECOGNIZE
ANY OF THE SONGS
OR SINGERS ON
THE JUKE BOX !!

GETTING IT ALL TOGETHER

i GET SO CONFUSED
SOMETIMES, i DON'T
KNOW WHICH END iS UP

....WHICH REALLY MAKES
iT DIFFICULT WHEN i TRY
TO SiT DOWN

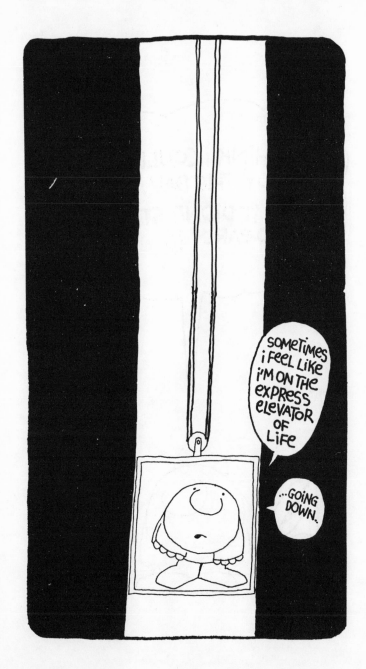

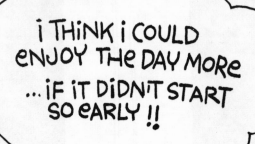

...i WONDER iF THERE'S A GREAT BiG "LOST and FOUND" iN THE SKY? ...WHERE EVERYTHING WE EVER LOST iS WAITiNG FOR US TO COME AND FIND iT.....

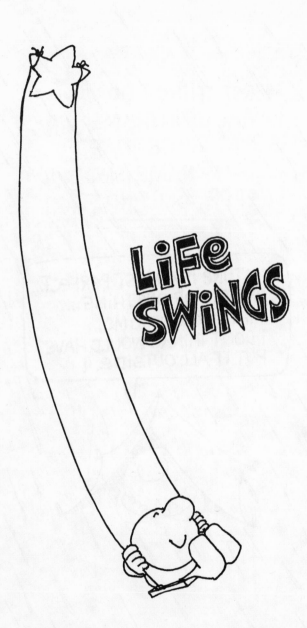

LiFe
SWiNGS

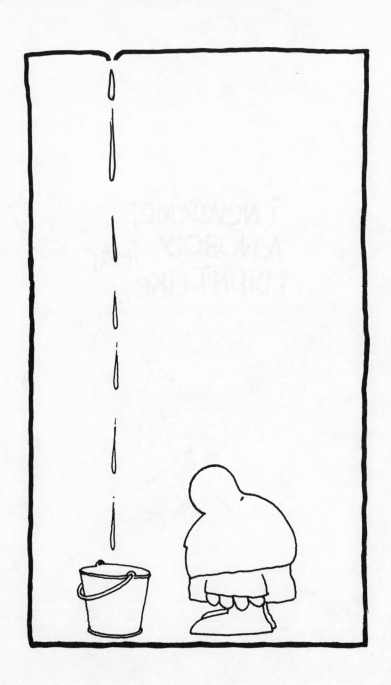

i NEVER MET
A NOBODY THAT
i DiDN'T LiKE...

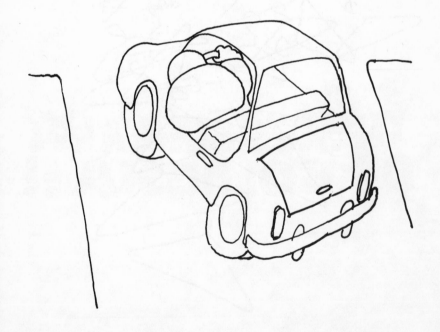

iN THE GREAT SANDWiCH of LiFe

THERE'S SURE A LOT OF BOLOGNA!!

OH WELL.. WE CAN'T ALL BE WINNERS

YOUR HIGHWAY
TAX DOLLARS
AT WORK

THE ONLY PLACE
i DON'T FEEL LIKE
A LOSER..
..iS ON THE
BATHROOM SCALES !!

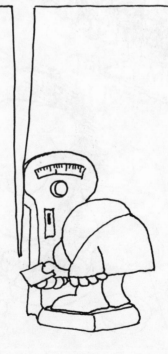

YOUR WEIGHT and FORTUNE

You made a pig of yourself over the holidays
...which leaves you with one of two choices
for the future:
1. Either lose 35 pounds
    OR
2. Grow 18 inches taller

GOOD LUCK!

YOU DON'T HAVE TO BE ALONE TO BE LONELY...
...BUT THAT'S WHEN YOU FEEL IT THE MOST !!
TOM WILSON

...THERE MUST BE A BETTER WAY TO SPEND MY EVENINGS THAN TO JUST SIT AROUND HOPING FOR A WRONG NUMBER...